CREATIVE TABLES

Whimsical Place Settings

To my beloved mother

Front cover: At the Farmers' Market table setting.
Back cover (clockwise from top left): Happy Birthday!, Tropical Paradise, Gardener for a Day,
Lights, Camera, Bon Appétit!, and Pretty in Pink tables.

© 2016 Assouline Publishing
3 Park Avenue, 27th Floor
New York, NY 10016
Tel.: 212-989-6769 • Fax: 212-647-0005
www.assouline.com
ISBN: 9781614285434
Translated from the French by Zachary R. Townsend.

Art direction: Paola Nauges & Jackie Shao
Editorial direction: Esther Kremer
Editor: Lindsey Tulloch
Color separation by Altaimage.
Printed in China.

BY ROSE FOURNIER
WITH THE COLLABORATION OF
SARAH AND PÉNÉLOPE FOURNIER

CREATIVE TABLES

Whimsical Place Settings

PHOTOGRAPHY BY YVES DURONSOY

ASSOULINE

CONTENTS

INTRODUCTION

I was born in the middle of a merciless and long-standing competition that began between my mother and my uncle: Who would be the best host? From the secret recipes each of them jealously kept to the finest tablecloth, everything was a question of rivalry. Creativity and refinement in my family have always been a very serious tradition, but more important, an entertaining heritage to carry on. Seeing the eyes of my family and friends filled with wonder when they discover a new table setting, as if it were a playground or a living painting, is my passion, expressed through the challenge to always be fun and surprising.

Entertaining can be a pleasure and a game, but it can also be a hassle, so it is important to focus on the basics, such as using a simple white place setting. Mine has become as familiar as an old, favorite pair of jeans—I use it for all my table settings. Decorating should come from inspiration of the present moment. Is it springtime? A family of cabbages on the table reflects the season. Today is your daughter's birthday? Anything from ballet slippers to math homework makes a perfect spontaneous centerpiece. Even an old box of pasta in the pantry can become a sophisticated and artistic arrangement. Courses served are matched with the decor and *voilà!*—ideas for creative tables that are simple and easy to organize.

But to be successful in such a challenge, there are rules to follow to help make it easier. Here are five essential ones to remember:

Rule #1: Always use the same set of white dishes to avoid the difficulty and expense of storing several different sets.

Rule #2: Use items already on hand. This is the perfect opportunity to revive old books from the attic or to find a new use for a child's paint set.

Rule #3: Purchase only the flowers, candles, and food.

Rule #4: Do not overthink it.

Rule #5: Have fun!

RM Fournier

DESSERT FIRST

Candy is not just for children: Thanks to its imaginative shapes and colors, it is an ideal accessory for any table. To avoid the feeling of a child's birthday party, the foundation of this table's decor is important. The Bordeaux wine–colored tablecloth brings a slightly dark and more mature mood to the look, while a sky-blue centerpiece and pale green placemats keep things bright. Here, placemats are paper maps of Paris, but any bright pastel paper will do.

Candy is not typically consumed in moderation, which is the intent, so it should be placed everywhere: a bowl of marshmallows for each guest, a lollipop and a candy necklace to bite on and resting in a nearby glass, and chocolate Smarties hidden in napkins—the candy is there to be savored. And for an adults' table, the candy should be playful, so edible paper becomes a writing surface for guests' names.

The centerpiece is composed of transparent containers to showcase the theme: a row of tall jars framed by two rows of glasses, all filled with candy, sorted by common color to avoid a gaudy effect or a juvenile appearance. This arrangement also places emphasis on the artistic shapes and soft textures that candy offers. Dining in front of a mountain of sweets implies that the menu will be colorful as well, echoing the sweet decor that the diners consume with their eyes.

A SWEET TOOTH'S MENU

Serves 6

Foie Gras Macarons
Spring Pea Soup
Oyster of Turkey with Spring Peas
Buttercream Cupcakes

Above: The brightly colored pea soup.
Opposite: This exciting table is reminiscent of a child's first trip to the candy shop!

KNIFE RESTS ARE A
HARD CANDY, AND EDIBLE
LIPSTICKS ARE PROVIDED
FOR EVERYONE IN CASE OF
A FASHION EMERGENCY!

CANDIES SORTED BY COLOR
ADD A TOUCH OF CLASS.

Top: A cupcake decorated with a frosted ladybug.
Bottom: Chocolate Smarties.

FOIE GRAS MACARONS

12 vanilla macarons

6 small pieces pre-cooked goose or
duck foie gras

o Separate the macaron shells, then place a piece of foie gras in the center and press the shells back together. Serve with a salad.

SPRING PEA SOUP

2 1/4 lbs (1 kg) fresh spring peas

6 1/3 cups (1 1/2 L) milk

Salt and freshly ground black pepper

o In a large saucepan, simmer the peas in the milk over medium heat for 15 minutes. Transfer the peas and the milk to a blender or food processor and carefully blend on low speed until smooth. Season with salt and pepper.

OYSTER OF TURKEY WITH SPRING PEAS

12 pieces turkey oyster meat (round, dark
meat pieces removed from the back)

1 Tbsp (15 mL) canola oil

1/4 cup plus 2 Tbsp (90 mL)
sweet soy sauce

12 3/4 oz (360 g) fresh spring peas,
steamed

Salt and freshly ground black pepper

o Brown the oyster meat in the oil on both sides, then let cook over gentle heat for 5 minutes. Add the soy sauce and cook for 1 minute longer. Serve immediately with the steamed peas. Season with salt and pepper.

o White sugar Mimosa balls (or small pieces of rock candy) can be placed on top of the peas.

BUTTERCREAM CUPCAKES

For the cupcakes:

3 large (150 g) eggs

1 1/4 cups (150 g) superfine granulated sugar

1 1/3 cups (160 g) all-purpose flour

1 tsp (5 g) baking powder

For the buttercream:

2 sticks (230 g) unsalted butter, softened

4 1/3 cups (500 g) powdered sugar

2 Tbsp (30 mL) milk

1 tsp (5 mL) vanilla extract

1 tsp (5 mL) green food coloring

o Beat the eggs with the sugar until lightened. In a separate bowl, sift together the flour and the baking powder, then beat this mixture into the eggs and sugar a little at a time, just until incorporated.

o Distribute the batter evenly in a greased cupcake pan and bake in the oven for 20 minutes at 350°F (180°C).

o Beat the butter until creamy. Add the sugar, milk, vanilla extract, and food coloring and beat just until incorporated.

o Pipe the buttercream on top of the cupcakes using a pastry bag fitted with a star tip. Serve with green chocolate Smarties.

AT THE FARMERS' MARKET

Summer is almost here, and with it come delicious veggies. They are the perfect accessories for a beautiful table—and so easy to find, so run to your local farmers' market and fill your basket with peas, plum tomatoes, asparagus, and peppers!

Green and red are the main colors for this table. The vegetables are chosen in these tones in order to avoid looking too messy or distracting. The tablecloth is white to allow the vegetables and green placemats to stand out. Glass containers are used to display the vegetables and showcase their beautiful colors and shapes. Mason jars or bowls may also be used here. A pot of basil and chives is added to the centerpiece. The yellow tulips, olive oil, red glasses, and bottles add a few pops of color to this fresh-picked table.

A MARKET MENU

Serves 6

Spring Pea Mousse and Garden Legumes
Spinach Ravioli with Two Sauces
Berries and Fromage Blanc

Above: Berries and fromage blanc.
Opposite: Details such as a miniature watering can make this table feel homegrown.

GENEROUS VEGETABLE CENTERPIECES GIVE THE ILLUSION OF DINING RIGHT IN THE GARDEN.

Left: Spring pea mousse and garden legumes. **Below:** Peas and tomatoes. **Opposite:** Asparagus, peppers, and celery as table decorations.

JUST-PICKED PEAS AND TOMATOES COMPLETE THE MEAL.

SPRING PEA MOUSSE AND GARDEN LEGUMES

8 1/2 oz (240 g) fresh spring peas

2 cups (50 cl) milk

1 lemon, halved

2 mini fennel bulbs, sliced

1 head iceberg lettuce

12 cherry tomatoes

6 chili peppers, for decoration

1/4 cup plus 2 Tbsp (90 mL) olive oil

o In a large saucepan, simmer the peas in the milk over medium heat for 6 minutes. Strain, then carefully blend the peas, along with the juice from one of the lemon halves, in a blender or food processor on low speed until smooth.

o Spoon into individual bowls and set them on plates. Garnish with the fennel, lettuce, tomatoes, and chili peppers. Drizzle the vegetables with the olive oil and a squeeze of lemon.

SPINACH RAVIOLI WITH TWO SAUCES

For the tomato sauce:

3 cups (690 g) diced tomatoes, with their juice

3 Tbsp (45 mL) olive oil

Salt and freshly ground black pepper

For the pesto:

1 oz (28 g) loosely packed fresh basil leaves

4 Tbsp (24 g) pine nuts

1/2 oz (14 g) grated fresh Parmesan cheese, plus more for finishing

1 garlic clove, peeled

1/3 cup (80 mL) olive oil

For the ravioli:

30 spinach and ricotta ravioli

o In a large saucepan, simmer the tomatoes in the olive oil for 30 minutes. Season with salt and pepper.

o In a blender or food processor, process the basil, pine nuts, Parmesan, and garlic until finely chopped. Continue processing and drizzle in the olive oil until smooth.

o Boil the ravioli for 3 minutes in salted water. Drain, then serve immediately with the tomato sauce, pesto, and Parmesan shavings on the side.

BERRIES AND FROMAGE BLANC

5 cups (1.2 kg) fromage blanc or Greek yogurt

10 1/3 oz (292 g) assorted berries

About 12 fresh mint leaves

o Spoon the fromage blanc or yogurt into bowls and arrange the berries on top. Garnish with the fresh mint leaves. Other toppings may be added to taste, such as honey, nuts, or white chocolate chips.

Opposite: Spinach ravioli with tomato sauce and pesto.

INCREDIBLE INDIA

Drenched in vibrant color and light, India is a fascinating place that, through its ornate objects and captivating stories, exudes a romantic fantasy. A bold table setting, which includes a sari, incense, religious statuary, and personal photographs taken while traveling there, represents the familiar and colorful traditions of a country that is also increasingly known for its modernity, as depicted by the rising stars and popular films of Bollywood. Who said traveling to a faraway land had to be complicated?

Leave behind the black and white motif of classic Hollywood, because here, the mot juste for this Bollywood table is color, and exclusively so!

An orange tablecloth is the foundation for pink cotton placemats. A sari in intense pinks is a must for this decor and serves as a table runner. Bright green napkins enhance the warm tones and further bring out the decor.

To tone down this color-saturated table, large hurricane vases are placed in the center, both right side up and upside down. Myriad objects, syrup bottles, and garlands of flowers are assembled on the table, and statues of Ganesha, the Hindu elephant god and protector of the home, are nestled in pink and orange sugar placed inside vases. The small colorful balls scattered on the tablecloth are sugar-coated anise seeds, traditionally eaten at the end of a meal in India.

Photographs are one of the most memorable and meaningful souvenirs from any trip. Locked in their frames or frozen in albums, they are easily forgotten; yet displayed under a vase or simply placed on the table, they make an effective element for the decor.

A BOLLYWOOD MENU
Serves 6

Carrot and Turmeric Soup
Chicken Curry
Mangoes and Coconut

Opposite: This table is steeped in vibrant tradition.

A SETTING READY TO WELCOME THE TASTES OF INDIA.

Above: An obsidian elephant decoration promenades across a napkin. **Opposite:** Color reigns supreme at this table.

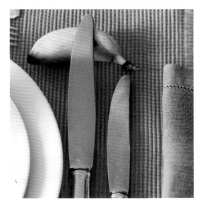  

CARROT AND TURMERIC SOUP

12 whole carrots
4 1/4 cups (1 L) milk
1 tsp (2 g) turmeric
Salt and freshly ground black pepper

o In a large saucepan, simmer the carrots in the milk and the turmeric over medium heat until tender, about 30 minutes. Transfer the mixture to a blender or food processor and carefully blend on low speed until smooth. Season with salt and pepper and serve.

CHICKEN CURRY

1 chicken, about 3 1/2 lbs (1.6 kg), cut up
    into large pieces
9 oz (250 g) onions, chopped
2 garlic cloves, crushed
2 Tbsp (30 mL) canola oil
2 Tbsp (7 g) mild curry powder
1 tsp (6 g) grated fresh ginger
1 2/3 cups (40 cl) coconut milk
4 ripe bananas
1 Tbsp (14 g) butter
1 pineapple, sliced
Mango chutney (from a jar)
1 1/2 cups (300 g) rice, cooked
Salt and freshly ground black pepper

o Brown the onions and the garlic in a skillet with 1 Tbsp (15 mL) of the canola oil. In a separate skillet, brown the chicken pieces over high heat for 5 minutes. Add the curry, ginger, coconut milk, and the cooked onions and garlic to the chicken. Bring to a boil, then let simmer for 30 minutes, covered.

o Slice the bananas in rounds, then cook them in the butter. Serve the bananas, pineapple slices, chutney, and cooked rice on the side with the chicken. Season to taste.

MANGOES AND COCONUT

3 coconuts, halved
3 mangos, cubed

o Fill each coconut half with cubed mango.
o Serve with your favorite chai.

Above, from left: The knife rests are real baby bananas; a fiery Ganesha statue; chicken curry. **Opposite:** Mangoes and coconut with chai.

PARIS
IS ALWAYS
A GOOD IDEA

Paris is my favorite city—no matter where I travel or where I live, it always feels like home. The look of this table is joyful, rich, and colorful, just like the city of light. From mini Eiffel towers to pastel paté cans and macarons, all these French specialties will make you feel like you are dining at a Parisian table.

The base for this table is a bright yellow cloth found at a market. There is no need to sew it into an actual tablecloth; tucking the extra fabric under the table does the trick. Green placemats are added over the yellow base to bring rhythm and depth to the setting. All of the objects picked for this table were chosen in a pink, green, and blue palette to give uniformity to the look. The flowers are light and a little messy. The pink Eiffel towers are displayed in transparent bowls and the candelabras are topped not with candles but real religieuses (custard-filled choux pastries)—the gourmands will be allowed a bite at the end of the dinner. As we say in France, it's all about *la joie de vivre*!

A PARISIAN MENU

Serves 6

Creamy Mushroom and Asparagus Vol-au-vent
Tournedos Rossini with Homemade French Fries
Religieuses Pastries

Above: Baguettes are an essential part of any Parisian meal. **Opposite:** Alongside the Eiffel Tower statue, the chandelier topped with religieuses becomes a monument to delicious Parisian pastry.

DESSERT IS EVEN MORE SATISFYING WHEN EATEN WITH A MATCHING SPOON!

8ᵉ Arrᵗ

AVENUE GEORGE V

Above: A religieuse pastry.
Opposite: Multicolored macarons are a decoration as well as a sweet treat.

CREAMY MUSHROOM AND ASPARAGUS VOL-AU-VENT

35 green asparagus stalks

20 portobello mushrooms

3/4 cup (20 cl) béchamel sauce
  (recipe follows)

6 vol-au-vent pastry shells

Salt and freshly ground black pepper

For the béchamel sauce:

1 Tbsp plus 2 tsp (25 g) butter

1/4 cup plus 1/2 tsp (25 g)
  all-purpose flour

1 cup (25 cl) milk

1 pinch nutmeg

Salt and freshly ground black pepper

o Snap off the tough ends of the asparagus stalks and discard them. Chop the asparagus and the mushrooms into small pieces and sauté them separately, well seasoned, over medium-high heat for 4 to 5 minutes or until tender; set aside and keep warm.

o Combine the cooked mushrooms with the béchamel sauce, then fill the pastry shells with the mixture. Add the cooked asparagus on top of the shells and serve immediately.

o In a medium saucepan, melt the butter over medium heat. Gradually add the flour while stirring with a whisk to smooth out any lumps between each addition. Cook the mixture over high heat for 2 minutes, then add the milk, a little at a time while whisking, until the sauce is smooth and creamy. Remove from the heat and add the nutmeg, salt, and pepper.

TOURNEDOS ROSSINI WITH HOMEMADE FRENCH FRIES

6 tournedos (filet mignon)

1 Tbsp (15 mL) canola oil

1/4 cup plus 2 Tbsp (90 mL) cognac

3 slices goose or duck foie gras (about
  3 1/8 oz/90 g each)

2 lbs (907 g) potatoes, such as
  Yukon Gold

3 3/4 cups (90 cl) vegetable oil
  for deep-frying

Salt

o Sauté the tournedos in the oil over high heat just until medium rare, about 5 minutes. Remove the pan from the heat, then add the cognac and ignite it using a long match; set aside and keep warm.

o In another pan, sauté the foie gras slices for 1 minute on each side, then place them on top of the tournedos.

o Cut the potatoes lengthwise into 1/8-inch-thick sticks using an adjustable blade slicer or by hand using a sharp knife. Transfer the potato sticks to an ice-water bath for 30 minutes. Heat the oil in a large heavy-bottomed saucepan until simmering. Strain and dry the potatoes, then fry them in the oil until golden, about 1 minute 30 seconds. Carefully remove the potatoes using a slotted spoon and set them on paper towels to drain. Season with salt.

RELIGIEUSES PASTRIES

o Pick up some religieuses from your favorite French bakery.

Opposite: Camembert is a fitting choice for authentic Parisian flair.

BACK TO BASICS

All city girls craved it at one point: escape to the countryside. Breathing the fresh air, walking through the green fields, eating organic for a day—there is nothing better than to reconnect with Mother Nature. But breaking free from a busy city life is not easy. So why not bring nature to your table?

A quick shopping spree at the local farmers' market and a huge bundle of green wheat stalks becomes the focal point of this table setting, ideal for reminiscing about peaceful weekends in the countryside. A rust-orange tablecloth brings out the green of the wheat bundle that rests elevated on several loaves of *pain de campagne* of various sizes, which add balance to the display. Grains of wheat are distributed around the loaves to complete the centerpiece.

This pastoral setting is complemented with a tall white dish filled with more grains of wheat, gold placemats at the ends and in the center of the table to help frame it, a faux-crystal candelabrum, and large red goblets. Tealight candles replace standard tall candles in the candelabrum, a small round loaf of raisin bread is placed on top of a candlestick, and bread plates are poised atop inverted egg cups, creating a table set to receive a menu inspired by nature.

Organic ingredients are selected where possible for this menu, with an emphasis on healthy choices. Refined objects and materials in sophisticated colors balance the rustic look of loaves of bread and wheat—what is natural can be glamorous!

A NATURAL MENU
Serves 6

Curly Endive with Wheat Germ
Spelt Risotto with Asparagus Tips
Pumpkin Soup
Panna Cotta with Strawberry Sauce and Pistachios

Opposite: From wheat to fresh-baked loaf, this table celebrates wholesome food.

RAW INGREDIENTS AND
THE FINAL PRODUCT ARE
PLACED TOGETHER ON
THE TABLE, ILLUSTRATING
THE BAKING PROCESS
FROM START TO FINISH.

Above: Cheese and berries round out the rustic menu.
Right: Wheat and bread. **Opposite:** Pumpkin soup.

CURLY ENDIVE WITH WHEAT GERM

1 head curly endive

7 oz (200 g) wheat germ

3 Tbsp (45 mL) olive oil

1 lemon, sliced into wedges

6 Tbsp (18 g) wheat germ flakes

Salt and freshly ground black pepper

○ In a bowl, toss the endive leaves with the wheat germ, then arrange the leaves on plates. Drizzle with the olive oil and a squeeze of lemon juice. Season with salt and pepper, then sprinkle the wheat germ flakes on top just before serving.

SPELT RISOTTO WITH ASPARAGUS TIPS

1 onion, chopped

2 Tbsp (30 mL) olive oil

1 lb (450 g) spelt

6 cups (140 cl) vegetable broth

2 1/4 lbs (1 kg) green asparagus

1 Tbsp plus 1 tsp (20 g) butter

3 oz (80 g) grated fresh Parmesan cheese, plus more for finishing

Salt and freshly ground black pepper

○ In a large skillet, brown the chopped onions in the olive oil over gentle heat for 5 minutes. Add the spelt, then stir for 2 minutes. Cook for 15 minutes while adding the broth little by little, waiting until each addition is mostly absorbed before adding more.

○ While the spelt is cooking, cook the asparagus for 5 minutes in boiling water. Cut off the tips and set aside.

○ Remove the spelt from the heat, then incorporate the butter and Parmesan. Serve with the asparagus tips and Parmesan shavings; season to taste with salt and pepper.

PUMPKIN SOUP

1 1/8 lbs (500 g) fresh pumpkin, peeled and roughly chopped

1 cup (250 mL) milk

Salt and freshly ground black pepper

○ In a large saucepan, simmer the pumpkin in the milk, covered, for 30 minutes or until tender. Transfer the pumpkin and the milk to a blender or food processor, then carefully blend on low speed until smooth. Season with salt and pepper and serve warm.

PANNA COTTA WITH STRAWBERRY SAUCE AND PISTACHIOS

2 cups (50 cl) heavy whipping cream

1/2 cup plus 2 Tbsp (125 g) granulated sugar

1 vanilla bean

3 gelatin sheets, or 1 Tbsp (9 g) powdered gelatin

10 1/2 oz (300 g) strawberries

Several whole pistachios

○ Combine the cream and 1/4 cup plus 2 Tbsp (75 g) of the sugar in a saucepan. Add the vanilla and bring to a simmer.

○ Meanwhile, soak the gelatin sheets in cold water. If using the powdered gelatin, sprinkle it over 1/3 cup (80 mL) of cold water and stir to moisten; let soften for 5 minutes. Squeeze the water from the gelatin sheets and add them to the warm cream (or add the softened powdered gelatin, if using) and stir to dissolve. Bring the mixture to a boil, then pour into small bowls and let cool for 5 hours in the refrigerator.

○ In a blender or food processor, process the strawberries together with the remaining 1/4 cup (50 g) of sugar until smooth. Pour the strawberry sauce over the chilled panna cotta and sprinkle with pistachios before serving.

Opposite: Spelt risotto with asparagus.

A FLORAL FEAST

Flowers are classic and enduring decorative elements that guarantee a successful table setting. Careful arrangement, however, is important to achieve the desired effect—rustic and unrestrained for a boho-chic look, colorful and well-trimmed for a more structured table, or arranged in flowerpots for a garden effect. As a break from vases, this setting includes daffodils removed from their pots and placed on small white plates. Flowers take over this table, seemingly transforming lunch into a picnic in a flowery meadow.

Yellow daffodils are the spotlight for this springtime table. To boost their intensely yellow color, a pale beige tablecloth and brown accents from paper placemats are ideal. Green napkins harmonize with both the color of the foliage and the green chamomile flowers in the bouquets. Buttercups, poppies, roses, chamomile flowers, daisies, and more yellow daffodils are presented in various ways in the table's center, with green tissue paper used to conceal the soil. Vases of different sizes vary the height and width of each arrangement.

Small bowls and short candlesticks hold tealight candles to disperse light around the table, as candles that are too tall would detract from the flower arrangements, which take center stage here. Green water glasses and small fanciful white goblets brighten the look of the white dishware. Hand-drawn place cards offer simple thoughts for each guest. To stay within this natural theme and to preserve the colors of the table setting, small leeks with vivid greens act as knife rests—it's important to make do with what is on hand.

A MENU FOR A MEADOW
Serves 6

Lettuce, Yellow Pattypan Squash, Pansies
Rack of Lamb with Beans and Cape Gooseberries
Rice Pudding and Daisies

Opposite: This setting is a feast for both the eyes and the stomach!

LETTUCE, YELLOW PATTYPAN SQUASH, PANSIES

18 yellow pattypan squash
4 Tbsp (60 mL) olive oil
Juice of 1 lemon (about 3 Tbsp/45 mL)
1 head lettuce, leaves separated
12 edible white pansies
Salt and freshly ground black pepper

○ Steam the squash for 4 minutes. Whisk together the olive oil and the lemon juice and toss with the lettuce. Season, then place the warm squash on top. Distribute a few pansies on top of the lettuce.

RACK OF LAMB WITH BEANS AND CAPE GOOSEBERRIES

1 or 2 racks of lamb (for 18 cutlets)
1 1/8 lbs (500 g) shelled beans, such as
    kidney beans
Several cape gooseberries
Salt and freshly ground black pepper

○ Preheat the oven to 425°F (220°C). Brown the rack of lamb, fat-side down, in an oven-safe skillet over high heat. Season with salt and pepper, then finish cooking in the oven for 25 minutes.

○ In a large saucepan, simmer the beans in salted water for about 30 minutes or until tender. Serve on the side with the gooseberries and the lamb, carved into cutlets.

RICE PUDDING AND DAISIES

4 1/4 cups (1 L) milk
1/4 cup plus 2 Tbsp (75 g)
    granulated sugar
1/2 cup (100 g) rice
6 edible daisies

○ In a saucepan, stir together the milk and the sugar, then bring to a boil. Sprinkle in the rice, then cook over gentle heat for 45 minutes or until tender. Serve with the edible daisies on top.

Above, from left: For a colorful addition to the table, serve a small plate of pâte de fruits with the rice pudding; lettuce, yellow pattypan squash, and pansies; dainty flowers decorate a tiny teacup. **Opposite:** Lamb with beans and cape gooseberries.

FLOWER ILLUSTRATIONS BRIGHTEN SOLID-COLORED NAPKINS, AND LEEKS ACT AS KNIFE RESTS.

Above: A flowery place setting.
Opposite: Floral-flavored candies may be added to the decor as an extra treat.

PRETTY IN PINK

What color is more feminine than pink? This all-pink-and-white table is ideal for a young woman's birthday. A white tablecloth avoids an overly girly look, and each guest is gifted with her own individual bottle of champagne, lending an air of elegance and sophistication to a motif of roses and hearts.

Tealight candles are placed in small vases to diffuse the light. For ultimate refinement, a candle in the shape of a religieuse pastry replaces a traditional candle set on a plate surrounded by the pastries—so Marie Antoinette!

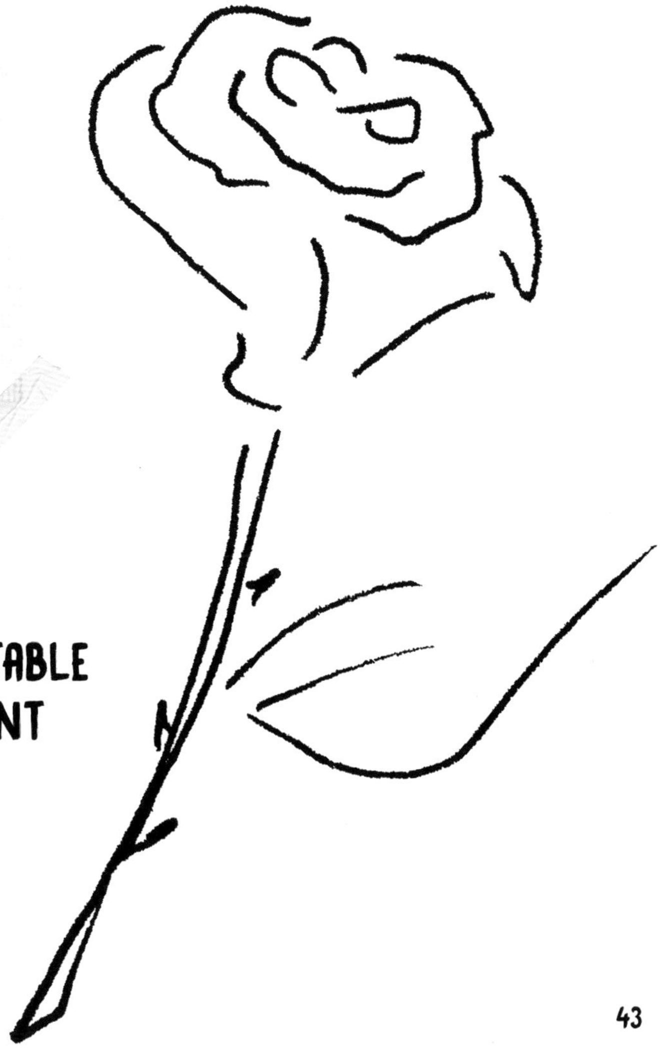

PRETTY IN PINK MENU
Serves 6

Tomato Gazpacho
Fresh Codfish with Broccoli
Religieuses Pastries

THE SHADES OF PINK IN THIS TABLE CREATE JUST THE RIGHT AMOUNT OF FEMININE FLOURISH.

Opposite: The key to a table in pink is adding complementary colors for balance.

TOMATO GAZPACHO

2 1/4 lbs (1 kg) tomatoes

1/4 cup plus 2 Tbsp (80 g) mayonnaise
    (recipe follows)

7 oz (200 g) croutons

1 green bell pepper, diced

For the mayonnaise:

1 large egg yolk

1 tsp (g) mustard

Pinch of salt and freshly ground pepper

1 cup (25 cl) canola oil

○ Process the tomatoes in a blender or food processor. Strain, then stir in the mayonnaise. Serve with the croutons and the diced bell pepper.

○ Mix the egg yolk with the mustard, salt, and pepper. Slowly drizzle in the canola oil while whisking vigorously, until the mixture is smooth and creamy.

FRESH CODFISH WITH BROCCOLI

6 fresh codfish fillets, 7 oz (200 g) each

1/4 cup plus 2 Tbsp (90 mL) olive oil

2 1/2 lbs (1.2 kg) broccoli

6 Tbsp (90 mL) sweet soy sauce

Salt and freshly ground black pepper

○ Season the fillets with salt and pepper, then cook them for 5 minutes in a skillet with the olive oil. Boil the broccoli; drain. Drizzle the soy sauce over the fish and serve.

RELIGIEUSES PASTRIES

○ Pick up some religieuses from your favorite French bakery. Serve with tea.

Above, from left: Codfish with broccoli; floral details are an essential part of this table; polka-dotted candles complete the look.
Opposite: A chic pastry-shaped candle adorns the dessert plate.

A STYLISH TEA SERVICE ELEVATES THE SCENE.

SERVE THE GAZPACHO, CROUTONS, AND PEPPER IN PINK TEACUPS FOR ADDED CHARM.

Above: A silver teapot.
Right: Tomato gazpacho with croutons and bell pepper.
Opposite: Flowers and fine teas perfume the table.

LIGHTS, CAMERA, BON APPÉTIT!

Black and white movies bring nostalgia for a day when our grandparents boasted of being chic and would imitate their favorite movie stars. While rummaging through my uncle's affairs, I found old film reels still in their large round metal canisters, a symbol of what was once the essence of Hollywood.

Black and white photographs of classic movie stars (John Wayne, Audrey Hepburn, and Rock Hudson, to name a few) are displayed on the table. A white tablecloth and black napkins are de rigueur, of course. Only very small touches of color—offered by traditional red roses, which represent the style of old Hollywood receptions—are provided a place among the reels and film strips. The movie canisters are converted into placemats, and strips of film are used as place cards. Dining in the midst of the classic Hollywood era brings such pleasure!

A HOLLYWOOD MENU
Serves 6

Cauliflower Velouté Soup
White and Black Blood Sausages with Turnip Puree
Chocolate Mousse

THIS TABLE FEATURES BOTH ON-SET AND BEHIND-THE-SCENES DETAILS.

Opposite: A setting with minimal color provides the ultimate glamour.

BLACK AND WHITE TONES RECALL SOME OF HOLLYWOOD'S EARLIEST MASTERPIECES.

Above: Cauliflower velouté soup.
Opposite: It's easy to imagine you're on the set of *Breakfast at Tiffany's* at this table!

CAULIFLOWER VELOUTÉ SOUP

1 head cauliflower
Scant 3 cups (70 cl) milk
Salt

○ In a large saucepan, simmer the cauliflower in the milk for 15 minutes or until tender. Transfer the cauliflower and milk to a blender or food processor, then carefully blend on low speed until smooth. Season with salt and serve warm.

WHITE AND BLACK BLOOD SAUSAGES WITH TURNIP PUREE

1 1/3 lbs (600 g) turnips, washed and peeled
3 1/2 Tbsp (50 g) butter
Scant 1/2 cup (100 g) crème fraîche
12 small black boudin (blood sausage)
12 small white boudin (blood sausage)
1 green apple, thinly sliced
Salt and freshly ground black pepper

○ Cut up the turnips and steam them for 20 minutes. Process them through a food mill or potato masher, then stir in the butter and the crème fraîche. Season well with salt and pepper.

○ Cook the blood sausages in a skillet for 10 minutes over medium heat. Serve with the turnip puree and slices of the green apple.

CHOCOLATE MOUSSE

7 oz (200 g) chocolate
3 1/2 Tbsp (50 g) butter
6 large eggs, separated
1 Tbsp (13 g) vanilla sugar

○ Melt the chocolate and the butter together in a bain marie, then stir in the egg yolks. Beat the egg whites with the sugar until stiff, then gently fold them into the chocolate mixture using a wooden spoon or silicone spatula. Let cool in the refrigerator for 2 hours before serving.

Above, from left: Blood sausages with turnip puree; Hendrick's Gin can be used to make classic cocktails enjoyed by the stars; chocolate mousse.
Opposite: Why not follow dinner with a film?

GARDENER FOR A DAY

Not long ago my husband decided to grow an herb garden, but our apartment has only five small window planters. In the midst of this crisis, he bought pots of thyme, chives, basil, and other herbs. After a fierce three-hour battle with the soil, fertilizing and watering, he decided that keeping a bouquet of chives, bought from the market next door, would suffice, so he left his collection of herbs in the kitchen. Not having the courage to let this little garden die, I decided to use it for a table. What a luxury to have a garden in the home!

In the center of this table, decorated with the color of apple green, the serpentine arrangement of pots of varying sizes avoids an overly rustic look. The color of the tablecloth echoes the color of the pots, while gold placemats provide the right amount of urban touch. Tags taken from the unfinished garden are used for writing the names of the guests, who also each receive a small pot of thyme, ensuring an abundance of greenery at the table.

A GARDENER'S MENU
Serves 6

Chilled Broccoli Soup
Basil Tagliatelle with Basil Sauce
Vanilla Ice Cream and Pistachio Macarons

Opposite: The herbs are the centerpiece here—in both the decor and the food!

CHILLED BROCCOLI SOUP

2 1/4 lbs (1 kg) broccoli
6 cups (1.5 L) milk
A few sprigs thyme
Salt and freshly ground black pepper

o In a large saucepan, simmer the broccoli in the milk with a pinch of salt until tender, about 20 minutes. Transfer the mixture to a blender or food processor and carefully blend on low speed until smooth. Season with salt and pepper, then place in the refrigerator to cool completely before serving. Garnish with sprigs of thyme.

BASIL TAGLIATELLE WITH BASIL SAUCE

3 oz (80 g) fresh basil
1/2 garlic clove
1 3/4 oz (50 g) fresh Parmesan cheese
3 Tbsp (45 mL) olive oil
1 1/8 lbs (500 g) basil tagliatelle pasta
1 small wedge (3 1/2 oz/100 g)
    Parmesan cheese

o In a blender or food processor, process the basil, garlic, and fresh Parmesan until finely chopped. Continue processing and drizzle in the olive oil until smooth.

o Cook the pasta in boiling water until al dente. Use a vegetable peeler to remove shavings from the Parmesan wedge. Place several shavings on top of the cooked pasta along with a spoonful of the basic sauce, then serve.

VANILLA ICE CREAM AND PISTACHIO MACARONS

o Pair pistachio macarons from your favorite French bakery with vanilla ice cream. A simple dessert for a meal in shades of green!

Above, from left: Plant tags make ideal place cards; chilled broccoli soup; even a small amount of herbs can add monumental flavor.
Opposite: Basil tagliatelle with basil sauce.

UNLEASH YOUR GARDENING GREEN THUMB IN THE KITCHEN WITH THESE VERDANT RECIPES.

Above: Yogurt with rosemary.
Opposite: Vanilla ice cream and pistachio macarons.

59

BABY'S BALLOONS

Table settings created for unique events, such as for a little girl's baptism as represented here, can be complicated: Too much white or pink can spoil a common convention unless a degree of modernity and maturity is imposed. Even though this celebration is in honor of an infant, it's the adults who are invited! Balance of the decor, therefore, is essential.

White napkins are selected for a brown linen tablecloth, which sets the tone and texture for this setting. Three unfolded white napkins anchor the centerpiece, where pink bottles of champagne, mandatory for the occasion, are placed (the tradition in my family is that you place a drop of champagne behind the ears of infants to bring them good luck). The decor is slightly relaxed and informal thanks to roses of different colors arranged in champagne flutes, as well as the use of mismatched candlesticks.

The napkin rings are a motif of simple ribbon to avoid the too-classic look of pink satin ribbon. The knife rests are wrapped pink candies, and a crown awaits the arrival of the little queen of the day. Balloons are attached to each chair and tied in a large cluster at the end of the table.

A BAPTISM MENU

Serves 6

Taramasalata

Marinated Salmon with Pink Peppercorns,
    Haricots Verts

Strawberry Ice Cream

BRIGHT BALLOONS ARE A SIGN THAT THIS DAY IS SOMETHING TO CELEBRATE!

Opposite: A baby's first celebration should be one the adults remember.

THIS TABLE CATERS TO BOTH
CHILDREN AND ADULTS WITH ITS
MIXTURE OF SWEETS AND DRINKS.

Above: Taramasalata with toasted baguette.
Opposite: Champagne in bottles of effervescent pink.

TARAMASALATA

1 1/8 lbs (500 g) tarama (codfish eggs), smoked and salted

Just over 3/4 cup (20 cl) canola oil

Juice of 1 lemon (about 3 Tbsp/45 mL)

○ Remove the eggs from their pouch. Using a mixer, beat the eggs while drizzling in the oil a little at a time until smooth. Mix in the lemon juice at the end. Serve with slices of toasted baguette.

MARINATED SALMON WITH PINK PEPPERCORNS, HARICOTS VERTS

1 1/3 lbs (600 g) raw, fresh salmon

Juice of 4 lemons (about 3/4 cup/20 cl)

1 1/3 lbs (600 g) haricots verts (string beans), steamed or boiled

3 Tbsp (45 mL) olive oil

2 Tbsp (20 g) pink peppercorns

Salt and freshly ground black pepper

○ Cut the salmon into 1/3-in (1-cm) pieces, then pour the lemon juice over them and let marinate for 10 minutes. Remove the salmon from the lemon juice and place on top of the cooked haricots verts. Drizzle with the olive oil. Season, then sprinkle with the pink peppercorns before serving.

STRAWBERRY ICE CREAM

○ What dessert is appropriate for a table where even the entrée is pink? Following the taramasalata and the salmon, a dessert of strawberry ice cream and red currants ensures consistency of the entire menu with the colors of the table.

Above, from left: Salmon with pink peppercorns; a baptismal crown; champagne bottles.
Opposite: Strawberry ice cream with red currants and madeleines.

CHIC WITH PASTA

Everything used for this table setting can be found in any kitchen pantry. Old boxes of dried pasta are an ingredient that never seems lacking. Here they become the stars of this table, which is complete without flowers or candles.

Even if it is a perfect replacement for flower bouquets, pasta still needs a vase to be effective. Its myriad interesting shapes are showcased using various transparent jars, pots, vases, and bowls.

Various clear containers are each filled with pasta of all kinds, from spaghetti to fusilli. Pasta is also transformed into real objects: penne used as knife rests and dried lasagna noodles used as place cards to inscribe guests' names. Small star-shaped pasta is strewn about the table.

A black denim tablecloth and white cotton napkins accompany the standard white plates—simple is beautiful.

Tradition demands that the Italian *primo piatto* be pasta! And for this table, the pasta should especially hold its own. Squid ink tagliatelle is a bold starter, looking so Chanel in black with white cream. Next, the calamari, artistically arranged on the plate, brings color to the table with its well-aligned green tomatoes—a light option after the pasta. Even dessert comes in black and white.

AN AL DENTE MENU
Serves 6

Squid Ink Tagliatelle
Calamari
Panna Cotta with Blackberries

Above: Squid ink tagliatelle.
Opposite: The decor and menu are so seamlessly integrated, it's hard to tell where the setting stops and the meal begins!

SQUID INK TAGLIATELLE

3 onions, finely chopped
3 garlic cloves, finely chopped
1/4 cup plus 2 Tbsp (90 mL) olive oil
About 2 Tbsp (24 g) squid ink
1/4 cup plus 2 Tbsp (90 g) crème fraîche
10 1/2 oz (300 g) plain tagliatelle pasta
Salt and freshly ground black pepper

o Brown the onions and the garlic in the olive oil. Add the squid ink and the crème fraîche, season, and set aside.

o Cook the pasta in boiling water until al dente. Lightly coat the cooked pasta with some of the squid ink sauce, with extra served on the side, and serve.

CALAMARI

1 1/3 lbs (600 g) calamari, cleaned
2 tsp (10 mL) canola oil
3 1/2 Tbsp (50 g) butter
Juice of 1 lemon (about 3 Tbsp/45 mL)
3 or 4 green tomatoes, sliced
Salt and freshly ground black pepper

o Cut the calamari into small pieces and brown them in the oil and butter for 5 minutes over high heat. Add the lemon juice and cook for 5 minutes longer over medium heat. Season with salt and pepper and serve with the tomato slices.

PANNA COTTA WITH BLACKBERRIES

5 gelatin sheets, or 1 Tbsp plus 2 tsp (15 g) powdered gelatin
Scant 2 cups (45 cl) heavy whipping cream
2/3 cup (15 cl) milk
3 Tbsp plus 1 3/4 tsp (45 g) granulated sugar
1 1/2 tsp (5 mL) vanilla extract
Blackberry preserves
36 fresh blackberries

o Soak the gelatin sheets in cold water for 10 minutes. If using the powdered gelatin, sprinkle it over scant 1/2 cup (10 cl) of cold water and stir to moisten; let soften for 5 minutes.

o In a saucepan, stir together the cream, the milk, the sugar, and the vanilla. Bring the mixture to a boil, then turn off the heat. Squeeze the water from the gelatin sheets and add them to the warm cream (or add the softened powdered gelatin, if using) and stir to dissolve. Pour the mixture into ramekins. Refrigerate for 4 hours.

o Just before serving, add some of the blackberry preserves and whole blackberries on top.

Opposite: Pasta is diverse enough to fill the table without candles or flowers.

CULINARY ARTS

My daughter Pénélope is an artist. Since she was a little girl, she has left her brushes, paint, pencils, and canvases everywhere in the house. One day Pénélope had been particularly creative (and messy!), and she came up with the perfect idea to avoid cleanup: create a beautiful table setting.

This artist's table is the result. Paintbrushes in hues of red-orange are intermingled with bouquets of flowers. After rummaging through Pénélope's art materials, I found sheets of drawing paper for placemats and various fabric swatches for added volume in the table's center. Every artist's material is used: boxes of pastels, tubes of paint, pencils, painter's palettes, and powdered dyes.

Guests' names are written on small notebooks in which they are asked to demonstrate their artistic talents—a sketch of a dream home or a portrait of a neighbor at the table, perhaps?

If crayons or brushes are casually arranged in their boxes, then they can be casually displayed in a glass, too. Are these paint brushes or bouquets of flowers? Bouquets of roses and cockscomb also lend an unusual velvety effect that brings warmth to the table.

AN ARTIST'S MENU
Serves 6

Feta Cheese and Green Pattypan Squash
Spring Chicken with Baby Potatoes
Apricot Tartlets

Opposite: A setting that whets the appetite for art.

FLAKY PASTRY

For a pastry worthy of this name, it's imperative to incorporate the butter thoroughly and correctly.

- In a large bowl, whisk together 4 1/3 cups (500 g) of all-purpose flour, 1 pinch of salt, and 2 Tbsp (25 g) of granulated sugar (or vanilla sugar).

- Using a pastry cutter (or a stand mixer fitted with the paddle attachment), incorporate 2 1/4 sticks (250 g) of softened butter, 2 large eggs, and several Tbsp of cold water, just until a smooth dough is achieved.

- Wrap the dough in plastic wrap and let rest for 30 minutes in the refrigerator before using. A good tip: This dough freezes well for long-term storage.

"LOGIC WILL GET YOU FROM A TO B. IMAGINATION WILL TAKE YOU EVERYWHERE."

ALBERT EINSTEIN

Above: Flavored syrups are reminiscent of paints.
Right: It takes merely the stroke of a brush for an artist in the kitchen to make this impressionistic feta cheese and green pattypan squash.
Opposite: A bouquet of brushes.

FETA CHEESE AND GREEN PATTYPAN SQUASH

36 green pattypan squash

1/4 cup plus 2 Tbsp (56 g) crumbled feta cheese

1/4 cup plus 2 Tbsp (90 g) crème fraîche

Salt

- ◦ Steam the squash for 4 minutes, then season with salt.
- ◦ Combine the feta cheese and the crème fraîche and serve on the side with the squash.

SPRING CHICKEN WITH BABY POTATOES

3 spring chickens (about 1 1/8 lbs/ 500 g each)

30 baby potatoes

Juice of 1 lemon (about 3 Tbsp/45 mL)

1 tsp (2 g) cumin

12 cherry tomatoes

Scant 1/2 cup (10 cl) water

Salt and freshly ground black pepper

- ◦ Preheat the oven to 400°F (200°C). Season the chickens, then place them in a baking dish. Add the potatoes, lemon juice, cumin, tomatoes, and water. Season again, then bake in the oven for 45 minutes. Serve warm.

APRICOT TARTLETS

1 recipe flaky pastry (see page 72)

20 apricots, quartered

6 Tbsp (132 g) apricot preserves

2 Tbsp (26 g) vanilla sugar

Crushed pistachios

- ◦ Preheat the oven to 400°F (200°C). Line tartlet pans with the dough. Place the apricot quarters into the pans. Brush 1 Tbsp (22 g) of the preserves on top of the apricots, then sprinkle them with the sugar. Bake in the oven for 40 minutes. Sprinkle the finished tartlets with crushed pistachios.

Above, from left: Apricot tartlets mimic the orange flowers, and a final touch of color comes from the pistachios; a cluster of crayons serves as part of the colorful centerpiece; the chicken and potatoes are presented theatrically, just as in the still lifes of the seventeenth century: a single roast chicken with baby potatoes and cherry tomatoes, served in a tall dish. **Opposite:** This table is an exquisite palette for your palate!

BUT FIRST, BRUNCH

Brunch is one of life's greatest pleasures, whether on a Saturday with girlfriends, a Sunday with family, or even on a weekday (which always seems a little forbidden and opulent). Everything should be permitted for brunch: biting into a chocolate croissant, then dipping its torn pieces into a soft-boiled egg; or champagne alongside coffee and orange juice. It's easy to see why brunch is such a favorite!

A pale beige tablecloth serves as the foundation for this brunch table, whose look is brightened for the occasion with apple-green placemats. The napkins selected are beige and match the tablecloth. Dressy white glasses complement the dishes, and clear glasses for the orange juice reveal a touch of color. The little rabbits, saved from Easter, help dress up the table; they are accompanied not by flowers, but by lettuce and leeks to avoid being cutesy. Frosted flakes, granola, and other cereals fill transparent jars, though any transparent containers, such as vases or bowls, would create the same tidy effect. And because brunch is a story of abundance, a pyramid of brioche buns is stacked in the center of the table. As an alternative to make-ahead Mimosa cocktails, each guest can receive a small bottle of champagne to pour into orange juice to make her own Mimosa. As stated in *The New Yorker*, "It's not brunch if it's not a drunk brunch!"

Anything goes for a brunch menu. Courses should be extremely simple to prepare to allow for a lazy morning where all cooking can be set aside. Food can be enjoyed in any order—soft-boiled eggs and small slices of toast with salmon roe, grapefruit sprinkled with sugar and quickly passed under the broiler, smoked salmon, sour cream and blinis, fruit preserves, and a plate of cheeses. Tea and coffee are an obvious essential. Casual ingredients, too, are always best, such as a simple pitcher of milk. Guests' names can even be written on the shell of each soft-boiled egg. There is nothing better than an easy weekend morning spent relaxing over a three-hour brunch.

A BRUNCH MENU
Serves 6

Soft-boiled Eggs, Roasted Grapefruit, Toast
Blinis with Smoked Salmon
Mimosa Cocktails

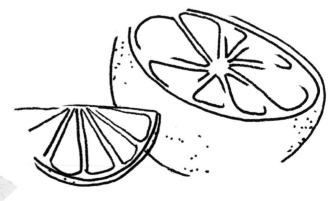

Opposite: Hopefully you can make room for a bunny brunch guest?

76

SOFT-BOILED EGGS, ROASTED GRAPEFRUIT, TOAST

For the eggs and toast:

6 eggs

A reliable egg timer

Any style bread, toasted and sliced

For the roasted grapefruit:

3 whole grapefruits

6 Tbsp (75 g) granulated sugar

1 tsp (2 g) ground cinnamon

○ For perfect soft-boiled eggs, immerse them in boiling water for 3 minutes only, and not one second more.

The Golden Rule:

○ For the best cooked eggs, remember the rule of 3-6-9: 3 minutes for soft-boiled eggs, 6 minutes for poached eggs, and 9 minutes for hard-boiled eggs.

○ Cut the grapefruits in half, then sprinkle each with 1 Tbsp (13 g) of the sugar and a little of the cinnamon. Place them in a baking dish under the broiler for 5 minutes.

BLINIS WITH SMOKED SALMON

Blinis

Smoked salmon

Crème fraîche

Fresh dill

○ Choose your favorite blinis and combine ingredients to taste.

MIMOSA COCKTAILS

1/4 cup (50 g) granulated sugar, to decorate the rim of the glass (optional)

Scant 1/2 cup (10 cl) champagne

1 cup (25 cl) orange juice

1 Tbsp (15 mL) Triple Sec or other orange liqueur

○ Lightly dampen the rim of the glass and dip it into the sugar, if using. Combine the champagne with the orange juice, then add 1 Tbsp (15 mL) of Triple Sec to taste.

Above, from left: A luxurious tower of brioche; roasted grapefruit; tea is a brunch essential.
Opposite: Blinis with smoked salmon, crème fraîche, and dill.

GAME ON

The atmosphere of a casino is dynamic, unique, and fascinating, with the bright colors, movement of the cards, sound of the spinning roulette table, players under stress, and the feeling of the dice and chips in one's hand. James Bond could casually sit at this table and order a vodka Martini!

The colors of this table dictate themselves: red for hearts and diamonds, black for spades and clubs, and green from table felt. To highlight the intense colors without bothering the eye, a pale beige tablecloth is used as the foundation for this casino-inspired decor. To augment the look of the linen tablecloth, silver placemats and white plates are accompanied by black napkins and a red rose—gambling can be glamorous.

The centerpiece consists of casino games arranged around a felt roulette mat. Clear dishes of varying heights allow a more interesting presentation of game pieces. Stacks of chips are used as knife rests, while the backs of heart-shaped cards serve as place cards. The whole room is best suited for dim candlelight. Dinner at this table could easily end in a fierce game of poker!

A GAMBLER'S MENU
Serves 6

Mâche Lettuce and Beet Salad
Cheese Soufflés
Pears with Caramel

THE DECOR ENSURES THE STAKES ARE HIGH
FOR THIS MEAL. LUCKILY THE MENU IS A WINNER!

Opposite: Home casino dining at its finest.

A LAS VEGAS-WORTHY TABLE.

Above: Feeling lucky?
Opposite: Using poker chips as table decorations
invites diners to follow up the meal with a game.

MÂCHE LETTUCE AND BEET SALAD

8 1/2 oz (240 g) raw beets
10 1/2 oz (300 g) mâche lettuce
4 Tbsp (60 mL) vegetable oil
4 Tbsp (60 mL) vinegar
Salt and freshly ground black pepper

○ Grate the beets over the lettuce. Season with salt and pepper. Whisk together the oil and vinegar and serve on the side.

CHEESE SOUFFLÉS

1/2 stick plus 1 Tbsp (75 g) butter
3 heaping Tbsp (30 g) all-purpose flour
2 1/2 cups (60 cl) milk
9 large eggs, separated
1 garlic clove, minced
7 oz (200 g) Gruyère cheese, shredded
1 pinch nutmeg
Scant 1/4 cup (5 cl) white wine

○ Preheat the oven to 400°F (200°C). Melt the butter in a saucepan, then whisk in the flour and milk. Continue whisking over gentle heat until thickened. Stir in the egg yolks, garlic, Gruyère, nutmeg, and white wine. In a separate bowl, beat the egg whites until stiff, then fold them into the Gruyère mixture. Distribute among ramekins and bake in the oven for 25 minutes.

PEARS WITH CARAMEL

6 ripe pears, peeled
1/2 cup (100 g) granulated sugar
2 Tbsp (30 mL) water

○ Place the pears in a saucepan and cover them with water, then cook, simmering, for 20 minutes.

○ Make a caramel by melting together the sugar and water. Cook without stirring until the sugar syrup turns light amber. Coat the cooked pears in the caramel.

To note:

○ As an extra treat, these are delicious served with shortbread cookies (see page 98) sandwiched with 1 Tbsp (20 g) of strawberry preserves.

Above, from left: A poker spinner is an appropriate and functional centerpiece; playing cards find a new use as place cards; pears with caramel and shortbread cookies with strawberry preserves. **Opposite:** Roll the dice on this cheese soufflé—you can bet it will be delicious.

LA VIE EN ROSE

"Je vois la vie en rose," sang Édith Piaf. This beautiful table is the perfect way to celebrate happy news or have a bachelorette party dinner in style.

The tablecloth is pink, of course. Green placemats are used to lighten this bright block of color. The centerpiece is made of delicious meringue pastries that can even be eaten for dessert. Upside down transparent dishes topped with plates allow display of the rose bouquets on each side of the centerpiece. The napkins are crinkled and placed in the glasses for a light effect. The key word for this table is "joy," so just sit back and see *la vie en rose*!

A ROSE-COLORED MENU
Serves 6

Pink Crayfish Salad
Marinated Salmon with Pink Peppercorns and Salicornia
Strawberry Mousse with Strawberry Sauce

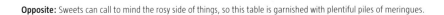

Opposite: Sweets can call to mind the rosy side of things, so this table is garnished with plentiful piles of meringues.

PINK CRAYFISH SALAD

18 boiled crayfish, tail meat only
1 grapefruit
2 ripe avocados
10 1/2 oz (300 g) mâche lettuce
1/4 cup plus 2 Tbsp (90 mL) olive oil
Juice of 1 lemon (about 3 Tbsp/45 mL)
Salt and freshly ground black pepper

o Separate and peel the crayfish tails. Peel the grapefruit and separate it into segments. Slice the avocados in half, remove the pits, then scoop out the flesh with a spoon and slice it.

o Place the grapefruit segments and the avocado slices on a bed of the lettuce along with the crayfish tails.

o Vigorously whisk together the olive oil and the lemon juice, season with salt and pepper, then drizzle over the salad.

MARINATED SALMON WITH PINK PEPPERCORNS AND SALICORNIA

1 1/2 lbs (700 g) raw salmon
Juice of 2 lemons (about 6 Tbsp/90 mL)
1/4 cup plus 2 Tbsp (90 mL) olive oil
1 cup (160 g) pink peppercorns
4 cups fresh salicornia
6 lemon slices

o Combine the lemon juice, olive oil, and peppercorns in a large bowl to create a marinade. Thinly slice the salmon and add it to the marinade.

o Boil the salicornia for 1 minute, then transfer it to an ice-water bath for 5 minutes to cool; drain. Transfer the salmon slices to plates, then garnish with the salicornia and lemon slices.

STRAWBERRY MOUSSE WITH STRAWBERRY SAUCE

6 oz (170 g) strawberries, hulled, chopped, and divided
1/2 cup (100 g) granulated sugar, divided
1 cup (25 cl) heavy whipping cream
3 large (90 g) egg whites
12 mini meringue cookies
Several sliced strawberries, for decoration

o In a blender or food processor, blend 1 cup (about 5 oz/143 g) of the strawberries, 1/4 cup plus 2 Tbsp (75 g) of the sugar, and the heavy whipping cream until smooth. Beat the egg whites to medium-stiff peaks, then carefully fold them into the strawberry mixture.

o In a small saucepan, cook the remaining chopped strawberries and sugar together while stirring, until the sugar is dissolved. Transfer the strawberries to a blender or food processor and carefully blend on low speed until smooth; set aside to cool.

o Place the mousse in individual bowls set on plates along with the meringue cookies. Serve the strawberry sauce on the side and decorate the plate with the sliced strawberries.

Above, from left: Strawberry mousse with strawberry sauce; a rose epitomizes the mood of this table; salmon with pink peppercorns and salicornia. **Opposite:** Pink crayfish salad.

TROPICAL PARADISE

For any parent with a full-time job who is always on the go, a vacation in the sun offers moments to celebrate. This table is the perfect reminder of tropical destinations. After returning from paradise, this setting can help ease the transition. It may be raining outside, but inside the feeling of being on vacation awaits!

A classic beige tablecloth contrasts with a Hawaiian shirt that is an essential part of the guests' dress code. The simplicity of this setting is elevated by green linen napkins. The centerpiece is composed of memories from paradise: a beautiful cluster of unripened coconuts, pieces of coconut tree bark, a bundle of cinnamon sticks, small seeds from an unidentified tree, whole nutmeg, and even a small, curiously shaped branch found on the beach. The large coconuts, potted orchids, carnivorous plants, and bananas were not carried home in a suitcase from the islands but were purchased from the florist and the market! Several candlesticks and a bottle of vanilla syrup placed on an inverted glass complete the look. A beautiful heart-shaped leaf resting on each guest's plate, chili peppers acting as knife rests, and just a bit of ground pepper next to small loaves of bread add a touch of color to the white place settings.

AN EXOTIC MENU
Serves 6

Crab Verrines

Swordfish with Sweet Potato Puree

Flambéed Bananas

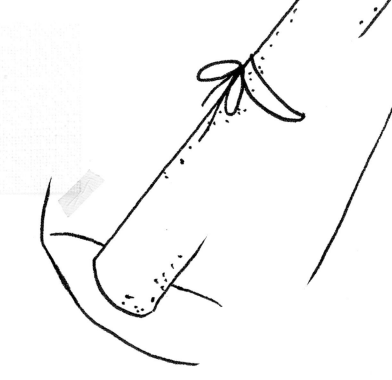

Opposite: Bring your hat—it's a supper safari!

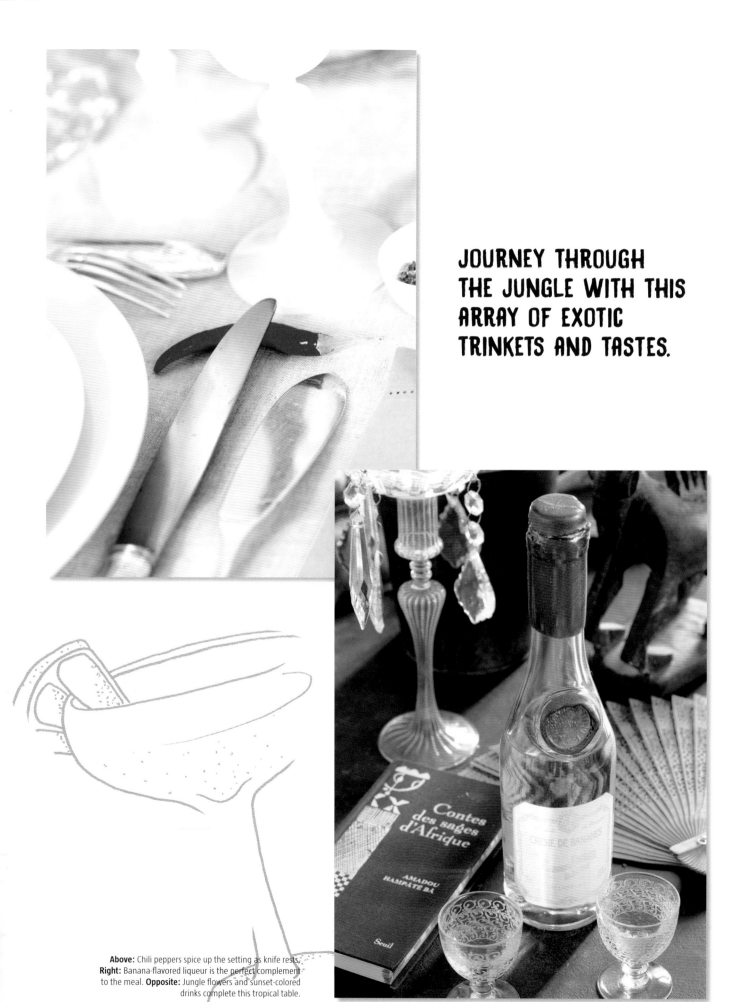

JOURNEY THROUGH
THE JUNGLE WITH THIS
ARRAY OF EXOTIC
TRINKETS AND TASTES.

Above: Chili peppers spice up the setting as knife rests.
Right: Banana-flavored liqueur is the perfect complement
to the meal. **Opposite:** Jungle flowers and sunset-colored
drinks complete this tropical table.

THE MENU FOR THIS TABLE COMBINES LAND AND SEA TO SWEET AND SALTY PERFECTION.

CRAB VERRINES

1 1/2 lbs (700 g) crumbled crab meat

1/4 cup plus 2 Tbsp (80 g) mayonnaise (see page 44)

Salt and freshly ground black pepper

o Carefully combine the crab and mayonnaise. Season with salt and pepper, then spoon the mixture into glasses. Serve with fresh tropical fruits.

SWORDFISH WITH SWEET POTATO PUREE

6 slices swordfish, 1/2 in (1.5 cm) thick

1 1/3 lbs (600 g) sweet potatoes, washed and peeled

3 1/2 Tbsp (50 g) butter

1 Tbsp (15 mL) canola oil

1/3 oz (10 g) grated fresh ginger

Juice of 1 lemon (about 3 Tbsp/45 mL)

Salt and freshly ground black pepper

o Cut up the sweet potatoes, then steam them for 20 minutes. Process them through a food mill or potato masher, then stir in the butter and season with salt and pepper.

o Heat the oil in a skillet. Cook the swordfish slices for 2 minutes on each side along with the grated ginger. Add the lemon juice at the end of the cooking time. Season and serve with the pureed sweet potatoes.

FLAMBÉED BANANAS

3 1/2 Tbsp (50 g) butter

6 ripe bananas, sliced in half lengthwise

Juice of 3 oranges (about 1 1/2 cups/35 cl)

1/4 cup (50 g) vanilla sugar

Scant 1/2 cup (10 cl) rum

Pinch of cinnamon

o Melt the butter in a skillet over gentle heat and cook the bananas for 5 minutes on each side. Add the orange juice and the vanilla sugar. Let simmer over gentle heat for 5 minutes.

o Just before serving, pour the rum over the bananas, then ignite them using a long match. Serve warm with cinnamon.

Opposite: Crab verrines with fresh mango.

BE MY VALENTINE

Leave the office early, light up a few candles, and turn your cell phone off: It's Valentine's date night. This table avoids the traditional, commercial red and pink tones. The soft greens and beige give the setting a more intimate look, complete with heart-shaped everything from name tags to bread and cheese. This table was created for Valentine's Day, but really, date night should be more than once a year!

The green placemats over the beige tablecloth create two definite spaces for this dinner date. The placemats are actually made of two open napkins, a useful trick to use what you already have at home. The large golden paper hearts placed next to the guests add a shiny touch. Two bouquets composed of green and white flowers are placed in the center of the table. They are cut low and purposely leave the middle of the table clear so the couple can gaze into each other's eyes. Love is in the air!

A ROMANTIC MENU
Serves 2

Asparagus and Foie Gras
Roasted Monkfish with Rice and Spinach
Heart-shaped Brie and Quince
Kiwis and Heart-shaped Shortbread

FORGET THE GUEST LIST—
THIS INTIMATE SETTING
IS JUST FOR TWO.

Above: Heart-shaped brie and quince.
Opposite: The perfect backdrop for a romantic evening.

ASPARAGUS AND FOIE GRAS

10 green asparagus stalks

2 slices goose or duck foie gras (about 3 1/8 oz/90 g each)

2 Tbsp (30 mL) store-bought Crema di Balsamico (balsamic cream) or high-quality, aged balsamic vinegar

Salt

○ Snap off the tough ends of the asparagus stalks and discard them. Boil the asparagus in salted water for 6 minutes. Cut out pieces of the foie gras using a heart-shaped cookie cutter. Serve with drops of the balsamic cream.

ROASTED MONKFISH WITH RICE AND SPINACH

2 monkfish fillets, 7 oz (200 g) each, skinless and boneless

2 Tbsp (30 mL) olive oil

Several sprigs fresh tarragon, chopped

1 cup (200 g) brown rice

2 oz (56 g) loosely packed fresh baby spinach

Béchamel sauce (see page 29)

○ Preheat the oven to 400°F (200°C). Place the fillets in a casserole dish and bake in the oven for 15 minutes. Add the olive oil and the tarragon on top; set aside and keep warm.

○ While the fillets are cooking, cook the rice in 2 cups (50 cl) of boiling water for 12 minutes or until tender. Spoon the rice into a heart-shaped cookie cutter to shape it for serving.

○ Make the béchamel sauce and set aside to keep warm. Boil the spinach for 3 minutes; drain. Add the spinach to the sauce and serve immediately.

HEART-SHAPED BRIE AND QUINCE

1 medium round of brie cheese

1 small container membrillo (quince paste)

1 oz (28 g) loosely packed fresh baby spinach

Vinaigrette dressing (recipe follows)

For the vinaigrette dressing:

1/4 cup plus 2 Tbsp (90 mL) olive oil

1 Tbsp (18 g) mustard

2 Tbsp (30 mL) balsamic vinegar

○ Using two heart-shaped cookie cutters of different sizes, cut out pieces of the brie and the quince paste. Toss the spinach with the vinaigrette; serve with the heart-shaped pieces of brie and quince.

○ Whisk the vinaigrette ingredients together in a large bowl until combined.

KIWIS AND HEART-SHAPED SHORTBREAD

2 ripe kiwis

3 Tbsp (42 g) butter, softened

2 Tbsp (25 g) granulated sugar

1/4 cup plus 2 1/2 tsp (29 g) all-purpose flour

2 Tbsp (18 g) almond flour

○ Cut the kiwis in half; set aside.

○ In the bowl of a stand mixer or using a hand-held mixer, beat the butter and sugar together until light and fluffy. Add the flours and beat just until incorporated. Wrap the dough in plastic wrap and press it into a disk; refrigerate for 15 minutes. Roll out the dough on a floured surface and cut out the cookies using a heart-shaped cookie cutter. Place the cookies on a lined baking sheet and bake at 350°F (180°C) for 10 minutes (the cookies should not turn brown). Serve with the kiwis.

RED AND PINK MAY BE ABSENT, BUT HEARTS ARE PLENTIFUL IN THIS VALENTINE'S TABLE.

Above: Hearts of all sizes, materials, and textures.
Right: Asparagus and foie gras with balsamic cream.

AT VOLTAIRE'S TABLE

Finding the right combination of gold without appearing too garish can require quite an effort. One answer can be found on bookshelves. A classic centerpiece will avoid gaudiness, and what could be more classic than leather-bound books? These quintessential centuries-old and universal objects can be picked up in antique shops, thrift stores, or perhaps even the attic. How about dinner at the table with Voltaire, La Bruyère, Descartes, or Molière?

Decorating in gold does not mean that all of the decor should be gold-plated. A bronze tablecloth is matched with the bindings of the antique books. The centerpiece is a strip of green linen fabric, and the placemats are made of solid gold (well, solid gold plastic!). Books that appear stacked or left open by a reader convey the warm, protective environment of a study. The rust-orange ranunculuses evoke the colors of the leather bindings and the tablecloth. Several bunches of flowers are placed in drinking glasses for a more intimate and toned-down setting; guests should be able to read passages of Voltaire without being obstructed by an arrangement. An abundance of candles provides the company experienced by readers of yesteryear. If using gold candles, opt for simple white napkins.

A WRITER'S MENU

Serves 6

Coddled Eggs
Seared Tuna with Lentils
Grapefruit, Vanilla Ice Cream, Ladyfingers

A SETTING FOR SCHOLARS.

Opposite: This table is transformed into a cozy, inviting study.

CODDLED EGGS

2 Tbsp (30 mL) heavy whipping cream
6 large eggs, separated
Red sea salt
Herbes de Provence

o Place 1 tsp (5 mL) of cream and 1 egg white into each ramekin.

o Place the ramekins in a bain marie and cook for 10 minutes on low heat, just until the egg whites begin to set. Thoroughly stir the cream and the egg white together. Just before serving, place the raw egg yolk on top of the mixture and sprinkle with the salt and the Herbes de Provence.

SEARED TUNA WITH LENTILS

1 1/3 lbs (600 g) fresh tuna
9 oz (250 g) lentils
Salt and freshly ground black pepper

o Slice the tuna into twelve large cubes and cook them in a skillet for 2 minutes on each side. Cook the lentils in boiling water until tender, about 45 minutes. Season, then serve with the seared tuna.

GRAPEFRUIT, VANILLA ICE CREAM, LADYFINGERS

3 or 4 grapefruits
1 quart (1 L) vanilla ice cream
6 pink ladyfinger cookies

o Halve the grapefruits and serve with ice cream and cookies on the side. This simple dessert blends in with the colors of the table.

Above, from left: Tea is the favored beverage for this subdued setting; the conversation at this table may turn naturally to classic literary greats; pieces of seared tuna bring a light element to the warm lentils, whose flavor can be enhanced if cooked with a small piece of salt pork.
Opposite: The colors of the coddled egg with toasted bread and the red sea salt echo those of the pages of the books and the orange in the flowers.

SPRING GREEN

Cabbages can be a beautiful representation of the arrival of spring. The decor for this extremely simple table comes straight from the market. Four pounds of cabbages of all varieties are placed on a table draped in a dark brown tablecloth. The only drawback to this theme is the amount of cabbage soup that must eventually be consumed!

To bring out the green color of the cabbages, several white tablecloths are scrunched around them as part of the centerpiece. Cabbages of different sizes create a certain harmony within their many proportions, and Brussels sprouts should be included for a more dramatic effect and to help hide the plain sides of the larger cabbages. To add a little whimsy and color, small candied eggs are placed here and there and served in small green bowls set on each plate. Spring is finally here!

A SPRINGTIME MENU
Serves 6

Baby Cabbages, Quail Eggs, Langoustines, Mayonnaise
Mackerel on a Bed of Cabbage
Mini Cream Puffs with Pistachio Cream

Opposite: Two candelabra flank the centerpiece of this table, each topped with a real egg.

BABY CABBAGES, QUAIL EGGS, LANGOUSTINES, MAYONNAISE

12 green baby cabbages
6 quail eggs, hard-boiled
30 langoustines, boiled
Salt and freshly ground black pepper

○ Blanch the cabbages for 3 minutes, then season with salt and pepper. Serve with the hard-boiled quail eggs, boiled langoustines, and the mayonnaise (see page 44).

MACKEREL ON A BED OF CABBAGE

6 mackerel fillets (from 3 mackerels)
1 1/8 lbs (500 g) kosher salt
1 green savoy cabbage, leaves separated
3 Tbsp (45 mL) olive oil

○ Cover the fillets with the salt and let stand in the refrigerator for 4 hours.

○ Rinse the fillets under cold water to remove the salt, then drain.

○ Boil the cabbage leaves for 10 minutes.

○ Place the fillets on the blanched cabbage leaves and drizzle them with the olive oil.

MINI CREAM PUFFS WITH PISTACHIO CREAM

1/4 cup plus 2 1/2 tsp (60 g)
    granulated sugar
1 oz (30 g) raw pistachios
3 Tbsp (45 g) crème fraîche
18 pre-prepared cream puffs
Chopped pistachios, for sprinkling

○ In a blender or food processor, process the sugar and pistachios until finely ground. Add the crème fraîche and process until smooth.

○ Place three cream puffs in each shallow dish on a pool of the pistachio cream and sprinkle with chopped pistachios.

Above, from left: Langoustines; baby cabbages and quail eggs; cream puffs with pistachio cream. **Opposite:** Mackerel with cabbage.

HAPPY BIRTHDAY!

Secretly raiding a child's room is an opportunity to find an abundance of items for a table setting that makes a perfect birthday surprise. Any object in the room is fair play for creating spontaneity—photos, ballet slippers, makeup, favorite books, a jewelry box, sunglasses, notebooks from an overseas trip, perfume, a pillow stitched with "LOVE" stolen off the bed, and even a bra are incorporated into this surprise theme.

Each borrowed item is staged on a colorful and cheerful tablecloth, which conforms to the mood of the evening. A large scrap of apple-green fabric (a remnant from my apartment curtains) and white plates are paired with pink napkins to keep this look bright and "girly." For a child whose sweet obsession is macarons, candles in the shape of these colorful confections are perfect for the occasion. Candelabra, adorned with the wax macarons, create volume and movement.

A SURPRISE BIRTHDAY MENU
Serves 6

Broiled Langoustines
Squab with White Button Mushrooms
Sabayon with Raspberries

Above: Personal and unique details from the birthday girl's life make this setting extra special. **Opposite:** There's no mistaking who this table is for!

"IT IS SURPRISING TO FIND THIS TABLE SETTING WITH PERSONAL ITEMS SO WELL STAGED. IT'S A GIFT THAT I WILL ALWAYS REMEMBER— THIS TABLE IS ME!"

MY DAUGHTER SARAH
ON HER NINETEENTH BIRTHDAY

A BIRTHDAY IS THE PERFECT TIME TO BE SURROUNDED BY PEOPLE AND THINGS YOU LOVE.

Above: Makeup and favorite chocolates.
Right: A pillow and pearls. **Opposite:** Ballet slippers.

NO BIRTHDAY PARTY IS COMPLETE WITHOUT SOMETHING SWEET.

BROILED LANGOUSTINES

24 langoustines
1 Tbsp plus 2 tsp (25 g) butter
2 Tbsp (20 g) anise seeds
Salt and freshly ground black pepper

○ Using a paring knife and starting from the top, split the langoustines open down the middle of the tail. Melt the butter with the anise seeds and pour it over the top of the langoustines. Season with salt and pepper. Place the langoustines in a baking dish under the broiler for 5 minutes and serve.

SQUAB WITH WHITE BUTTON MUSHROOMS

6 squab (domestic pigeon)
7 oz (200 g) lardons (thick-cut bacon, cut into small cubes)
9 oz (250 g) white button mushrooms, thinly sliced
1 Tbsp (15 mL) canola oil
1 head garlic
Salt and freshly ground black pepper

○ Brown the lardons in a skillet. Add the mushrooms to the pan and cook over gentle heat for 10 minutes, then set aside.

○ Brown the squab in a Dutch oven with the oil. Add the lardons, cooked mushrooms, head of garlic, and about 2 cups (50 cl) of water. Season and let simmer for 30 minutes or until cooked through. Adjust the seasoning as needed before serving.

SABAYON WITH RASPBERRIES

6 large (112 g) egg yolks
3/4 cup plus 1 Tbsp (170 g) granulated sugar
1 1/4 cups (30 cl) Marsala wine
9 oz (250 g) raspberries

○ In a bowl, whisk together the egg yolks and sugar until lightened. Whisk in the Marsala wine. Cook the mixture over very low heat, whisking constantly, until very thick.

○ Immediately spoon the sabayon into bowls. Add the raspberries on top and serve.

Opposite: The sabayon with raspberries is an especially eye-catching dessert.

AUTUMN HARVEST

Don't you love it when nature shifts into its autumn colors and everything turns red, orange, and purple? During this season, every detail is a source of inspiration, from the leaves on the ground to the purple grapes ready for harvest. Perfect for a beautiful table!

The dark purple cloth makes the ideal base for this Autumn-themed table. The green placemats bring a touch of light to the setting and match the green cloth used for the centerpiece. Pink napkins add an additional pop of color. Empty vases, bowls, and glasses placed under and over the fabric create different heights and volumes at the center of the table. Seasonal products become the highlight, from a bright green cabbage to a simple yet beautiful broccoli. Even red onions, displayed on upside down glasses, look almost like precious jewels.

A FALL MENU

Serves 6

Cabbage Mousse with Fresh Apple

Oak Leaf Salad

Oyster of Turkey with Red Cabbage
  and Creamy Mashed Potatoes

Roasted Figs

Opposite: An homage to the bounty of fall.

A HEARTY MEAL TO WELCOME THE COOLER MONTHS.

Above: Oyster of turkey with red cabbage and mashed potatoes.
Opposite: Onions receive a place of honor as treasures from the harvest.

THE APPLE AND PINE NUTS,
PLUS BLACK SEA SALT,
COMPLEMENT THE SUBTLE
FLAVOR OF THE MOUSSE.

THE ROASTED FIG EMBODIES
AN AUTUMN SUNSET.

Above: Cabbage mousse with apple slices.
Right: Roasted fig with pecans.

CABBAGE MOUSSE WITH FRESH APPLE

1/2 head red cabbage

4 cups (100 cl) milk

1 apple, thinly sliced

1 Tbsp (8 g) pine nuts

Black sea salt

Salt and freshly ground black pepper

o Cut up the cabbage into large pieces and simmer it in the milk over low heat for 20 minutes. Transfer the milk and cabbage to a blender or food processor, season with salt and pepper, then carefully blend on low speed until smooth. Serve warm with the apple slices on top and a sprinkle of toasted pine nuts and black sea salt.

OAK LEAF SALAD

1 head oak leaf lettuce

Vinaigrette dressing (see page 98)

6 scallions, chopped

Salt and freshly ground black pepper

o Clean and wash the lettuce, then separate the leaves. Toss the lettuce with the vinaigrette. Add the chopped scallions and season with salt and pepper.

OYSTER OF TURKEY WITH RED CABBAGE AND CREAMY MASHED POTATOES

12 pieces turkey oyster meat (round, dark meat pieces removed from the back)

1 Tbsp (15 mL) canola oil

1/2 head red cabbage

2 Tbsp (26 g) brown sugar

1 Tbsp (15 mL) balsamic vinegar

6 small potatoes, washed, peeled, and cut into large pieces

Scant 1 cup (20 cl) milk

1/2 stick plus 1 Tbsp (70 g) butter

Salt and freshly ground black pepper

o Brown the oyster meat in the oil on both sides, then let cook over gentle heat for 5 minutes.

o Boil the cabbage with the sugar and vinegar in 3 cups (75 cl) of water for 20 minutes.

o In a large saucepan, simmer the potatoes in the milk, covered, for 20 minutes; drain, reserving the milk. Mash the potatoes with a fork while slowly incorporating the milk and the butter. Season with salt and pepper.

ROASTED FIGS

6 fresh figs

1/4 cup plus 2 Tbsp (90 mL) store-bought Crema di Balsamico (balsamic cream) or high-quality, aged balsamic vinegar

1/4 cup plus 2 Tbsp (75 g) granulated sugar

20 pecans

6 vanilla beans, for decoration

o Preheat the oven to 400°F (200°C). Cut the figs into quarters. Place them in a casserole dish and bake in the oven for 5 minutes.

o In a small saucepan, warm the balsamic cream and the sugar over low heat; stir until the sugar has dissolved. Pour over the figs and serve with pecans and a vanilla bean on the side.

MERRY
CHRISTMAS!

A Christmas table is always a challenge. The theme is not new, and, above all, its staging must be grand. Presents were selected as the theme for this table to best celebrate this magical holiday, as collections of wrapping paper stored in the closet are underrated as elements for decor.

The hues selected for this Christmas table are gold and white over the traditional red, giving other classic colors a chance to shine. Gold placemats surround the centerpiece. Crumpled pieces of white and gold tissue paper create a simple centerpiece that is recycled yet ethereal and spectacular. A garland of string lights entwined under the wrapping paper creates even more wonder and magic.

Another Christmas essential: ornaments, which are scattered on the tissue paper and made into napkin rings using just one bow and one ornament from the tree. White and gold Christmas tree candles (replaced today by electric string lights) fill the table and are set within candlesticks and candle holders of varying heights and styles, further illuminating the magic of Christmas.

A CHRISTMAS MENU
Serves 6

Crayfish Verrines
Lobster with Melted Butter
Foie Gras and Haricots Verts
Baked Apples

A GOLDEN TABLE THAT GLIMMERS LIKE THE STAR ON TOP OF THE TREE.

Above: Crayfish verrines.
Opposite: This setting elegantly captures the holiday's warm glow.

'TIS THE SEASON TO BE CREATIVE WITH YOUR DECORATIONS!

Above: Even the napkins are gifts at this magical table.
Opposite: Baked apple with cinnamon, Christmas cookie, and quince jelly.

CRAYFISH VERRINES

6 boiled crayfish, tail meat only

3 gelatin sheets, or 1 Tbsp (9 g) powdered gelatin

Scant 1/2 cup (10 cl) consommé (clarified broth), warmed

Scant 1/2 cup (100 g) crème fraîche, softened just until liquid

○ Soak the gelatin sheets in cold water. If using the powdered gelatin, sprinkle it over 1/3 cup (80 mL) of cold water and stir to moisten; let soften for 5 minutes. Squeeze the water from the gelatin sheets and add them to the warm consommé (or add the softened powdered gelatin, if using) and stir to dissolve.

○ Place one crayfish tail in each glass, then cover it with the consommé. Place in the refrigerator until set, then pour 1 tsp (5 mL) of the crème fraîche into each glass.

LOBSTER WITH MELTED BUTTER

6 lobsters

Butter, melted

○ Boil the lobsters, then serve them with the melted butter on the side.

FOIE GRAS AND HARICOTS VERTS

1 goose or duck foie gras, 1 1/3 lbs (600 g)

1 Tbsp (15 mL) port wine

1 Tbsp (15 mL) sherry vinegar

Salt

12 2/3 oz (360 g) haricots verts (string beans), steamed or boiled

○ Remove the foie gras from the refrigerator 2 hours in advance to make deveining it easier. Preheat the oven to 240°F (120°C). Devein the foie gras, then season it with salt and place it in a terrine. Pour the port and sherry into the terrine, then press the foie gras down into the terrine to fit snugly. Bake in the oven for 35 minutes. Serve with the cooked haricots verts.

BAKED APPLES

6 large baking apples, such as Granny Smith

6 tsp (25 g) granulated sugar

Ground cinnamon

○ Preheat the oven to 350°F (180°C). Place the apples in a baking dish and sprinkle each one with 1 tsp (4 g) of the sugar. Pour a scant 1/2 cup (100 mL) water into the dish. Bake in the oven for 20 minutes. Sprinkle the apples with cinnamon just before serving.

Opposite: Lobster with melted butter.

NEW YEAR'S EVE

New Year's, just like Christmas, is a difficult theme. It calls for shiny tones that can quickly turn into an overdose of "bling." This table stays at a safe distance from golds and silvers and uses white to transition into the New Year.

A simple white tablecloth topped with white wrapping paper in the center of the table creates a snowy look. A few mini Christmas trees and white bottles of champagne finish the centerpiece. To avoid being too theatrical, small candles are a good alternative for the candelabra. The black napkins are topped with ornaments taken down from the Christmas tree. Finish the look with star-shaped cookies and this table is ready for countdown!

A MENU FOR THE NEW YEAR
Serves 6

Hot and Cold Cauliflower Mousse
Truffle Risotto
Chocolate Fondant

A CLEAN WHITE REPRESENTS A FRESH START FOR THE COMING YEAR.

Opposite: A dusting of snow on this table welcomes the New Year.

HOT AND COLD CAULIFLOWER MOUSSE

1/2 head cauliflower
4 cups (100 cl) milk
1 small black truffle

o Chop the cauliflower into large pieces. Set aside six small pieces for finishing, then simmer the remaining pieces in the milk over low heat for 20 minutes. Transfer the cauliflower pieces and milk to a blender or food processor and carefully process on low speed until smooth. Serve with a piece of raw cauliflower and thin slices of truffle on top.

TRUFFLE RISOTTO

1 stick (113 g) butter, cut up and
    equally divided
2 1/2 cups (500 g) arborio rice
4 cups (100 cl) beef broth
3/4 oz (21 g) grated fresh
    Parmesan cheese
1 small black truffle

o Melt half of the butter in a skillet, then add the rice. Cook over medium heat, stirring, until the rice has become transparent. Gradually add the broth while continuing to stir, waiting until the rice absorbs the broth after each addition (about 1 ladleful with each addition; this will take about 20 minutes). When the rice is tender and the liquid has been fully absorbed, stir in the remaining butter, then stir in the Parmesan. Spoon into ring molds to serve, then add truffle shavings on top.

CHOCOLATE FONDANT

6 oz (170 g) dark chocolate
1 cup (200 g) granulated sugar
1 1/2 sticks plus 1 Tbsp (184 g) butter
5 large (250 g) eggs
1/4 cup plus 1/2 tsp (25 g)
    all-purpose flour

o Preheat the oven to 375°F (190°C). Melt the chocolate, sugar, and butter together in a bain marie. Let cool, then whisk in the eggs one at a time. Add the flour and whisk until smooth. Pour into greased individual brioche or cupcake molds and bake in the oven for 20 minutes (do not overbake). Let cool in the pans for 10 minutes, then turn out and serve.

Above, from left: Chocolate fondant; a tiny star cookie decoration; cauliflower mousse. **Opposite:** Truffle risotto.

RECIPE INDEX

ACKNOWLEDGMENTS

I would like to thank my two daughters: Pénélope, who drew the delicate illustrations that represent my passion, and Sarah, who translated within the text, with great skill, everything that I wanted to express; Leonard, who supported, loved, and encouraged me every step of the way; Nathalie Degrèes du Loû, my longtime partner in crime; Agnès Malabanan, my precious collaborator; Léon Jerusalmi, Maurice de Toledo, Martine Chiche, Suzy Rémi, and Francine Hardy, who taught me passion for beautiful things, details, and refinement; Ugo Barbaresco, my eternal guardian angel; Elena Barbaresco, Paulette Gherman, Paulette Pinhas, and Henriette Ojalvo, who taught me the pleasure of cooking; Vicky Loria, who ate countless cheese soufflés with me when I was a little girl; Nora Sabrier, who introduced me to her editor; Dominique Fournier, for his support; Yves Duronsoy, a talented photographer who accompanied me during this great adventure; and Nathalie Amsellem, who helped me develop this project.

Assouline would like to thank Rose Fournier and her family for their collaboration and creativity, as well as Nora Sabrier for her kind introduction. Thank you to Esther Kremer, Paola Nauges, Jackie Shao, Lindsey Tulloch, Zach Townsend, Andrea Chlad, Stephanie Umeda, and Stephanie Handy for their invaluable work on this book.

Rose Fournier is a designer and a writer. Born in Paris and brought up in the exuberance of hosting and entertaining, she developed her talent for the art of the table from family traditions. Her shared passions for decorating, cooking, and traveling impart constant creativity and culinary variety into her settings, which she creates with efficacy and simplicity.

Yves Duronsoy was born in Paris. A self-taught photographer, he began his career as a photojournalist, shooting in black and white. His interests include fashion and portrait photography, decorating, and *art de vivre*—always with a desire to "convey a look without pretense." He has collaborated on numerous fashion and decorating magazines and has photographed for brands including Habitat, Hermès, and Baccarat, as well as Le Bon Marché and Printemps department stores. He has also contributed to several books on photography and the art of living. The use of natural light and the desire to capture the mood of a moment are the driving forces behind his photography.